WHEELS & AXLES

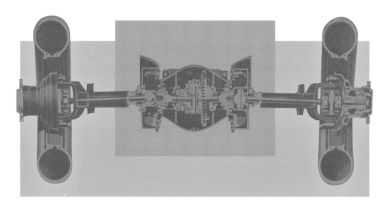

A Buddy Book

by

sarah tieck

ABDO
Publishing Company

Published by ABDO Publishing Company, 4940 Viking Drive, Edina, Minnesota 55435.

Contributing Editor: Michael P. Goecke
Graphic Design: Maria Hosley
Cover Photograph: Photos.com, Clipart.com
Interior Photographs/Illustrations: Clipart.com, Fotosearch, Photos.com, Professional Litho

Library of Congress Cataloging-in-Publication Data

Tieck, Sarah, 1976–
    Wheels and axles / Sarah Tieck.
      p. cm. — (Simple machines)
    Includes index.
    ISBN-13: 978-1-59679-819-9
    ISBN-10: 1-59679-819-X
    1. Wheels—Juvenile literature. 2. Axles—Juvenile literature. I. Title II. Series: Tieck, Sarah, 1976- Simple machines.

TJ181.5.T54 2006
621.8—dc22

                                          2006010048

Table Of Contents

What Is A Wheel And Axle?

The wheel and axle is used to move things more easily. A wheel and axle is a simple machine. A simple machine has few moving parts, sometimes only one.

Simple machines give people a mechanical advantage. This is how the wheel and axle helps make work easier for people.

4

Ferris wheels move easily because of the wheel and axle.

The wheel and axle is not the only simple machine. There are six simple machines. These include wheels and axles, wedges, levers, pulleys, screws, and inclined planes.

Sometimes, simple machines work together. Most machines are made up of more than one simple machine. Examples of wheels and axles include doorknobs, clock parts, and car wheels.

simple machines

Inclined Planes
Help move objects.

Levers
Help lift or move objects.

Pulleys
Help move, lift, and lower objects.

Screws
Help lift, lower, and fasten objects.

Wedges
Help fasten or split objects.

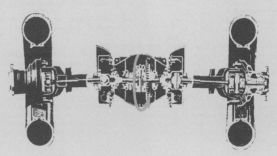

Wheels and Axles
Help move objects.

Parts Of A Wheel And Axle

The wheel and axle work together to help move things.

A wheel and axle is made up of two main parts. There is a large circular piece on the outside. This is the wheel. On the inside, is the axle. Many times, the axle looks like a rod. The wheel and axle turn together.

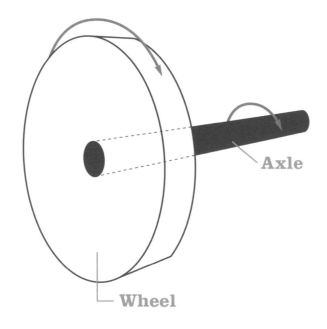

Axle

Wheel

Someone or something must supply force to turn the wheel. This force is what makes the wheel and axle work. When the wheel is turned, the axle turns, too.

HOW Does A Wheel And Axle Work?

Most people can probably move a bucket full of water on their own. But, this same job would be easier with the help of a wheel and axle.

The wheel and axle makes work easier. This is because the wheel and axle gives a person a mechanical advantage.

Wheel
The crank is attached to the wheel.
It makes the wheel easy to turn.

Axle
The rope is attached to the axle.

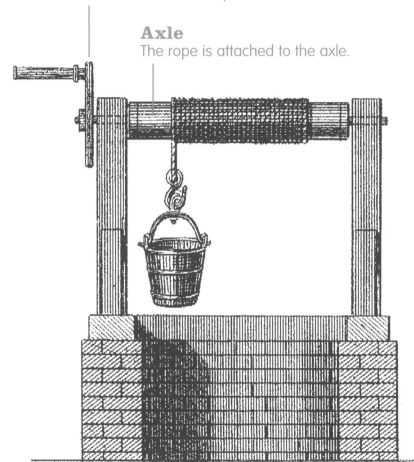

A person can use a wheel and axle to get a bucket of water from a well. First, he or she would tie one end of a rope around the bucket. Then, they would tie the rope's other end around the axle.

To lower the bucket into the water, that person would turn the wheel and axle using a crank. The crank helps provide **force** to move the wheel and axle. This action will also help bring the bucket of water back up from the well.

The crank is on the wheel. When the crank is turned, the wheel and axle turn, too. This causes the rope to wind around the axle.

Different Wheels And Axles At Work

There are many different ways to use a wheel and axle. It is possible to change the way a wheel and axle moves. It is also possible to change the shape, size, or angle of a wheel and axle.

These changes help this simple machine perform different jobs. Because of this, the wheel and axle has many uses.

A child's toy wagon is built on top of wheels and axles. The wheels and axles help the wagon to move more easily.

A wagon rolls because of the wheel and axle. The axles help to attach the body of the wagon to the wheels. The outer wheels help someone to move the wagon along.

Larger wheels make moving things easier than smaller wheels. Larger wheels give a greater **mechanical advantage**.

A manual pencil sharpener uses a crank to turn the wheel and axle.

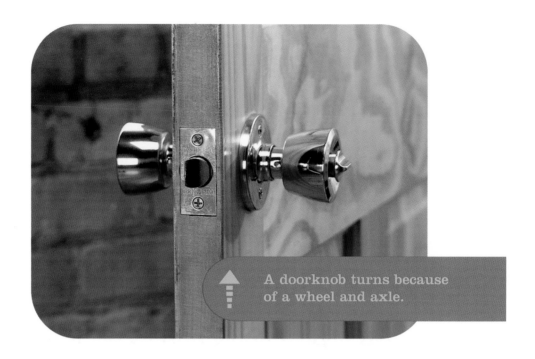

A doorknob turns because of a wheel and axle.

A doorknob is also an example of a wheel and axle. The axle goes through the hole in the door. The doorknob is the outer wheel. The doorknob and axle turn together. Larger knobs, or larger wheels, require less **effort** to turn than smaller ones.

Tricycle pedals are cranks.

A tricycle uses wheels and axles, too. A tricycle has one large wheel in the front. This wheel is attached to the tricycle's frame by an axle. There are two smaller wheels and axles in the back.

The tricycle's big wheel moves because of a crank. Using the crank helps provide force to move the wheels and axles.

The History Of Wheels And Axles

The wheel and axle has been used for many years. It was one of the first tools and was used by early people.

In ancient times, people didn't have machines with motors. They had to do work with their bodies. They moved many things by hand.

It is said that these ancient people used the wheel and axle to help them move things. The wheel and axle helped make ancient people's work easier. This tool is still used today.

One ancient version of the wheel and axle was a log. The log helped early people move objects.

How Do Wheels And Axles Help People Today?

Today people have many types of tools, but they still use the wheel and axle.

When you pedal a bicycle, it moves because of a wheel and axle. When you use a clock to tell time, a wheel and axle helps the clock's hands move. When you ride on a ferris wheel at an amusement park, that is another example of a wheel and axle.

A shopping cart (top left), a tricycle (top right), a go-kart (bottom left), and a ferris wheel (bottom right) in motion are all examples of the wheel and axle at work.

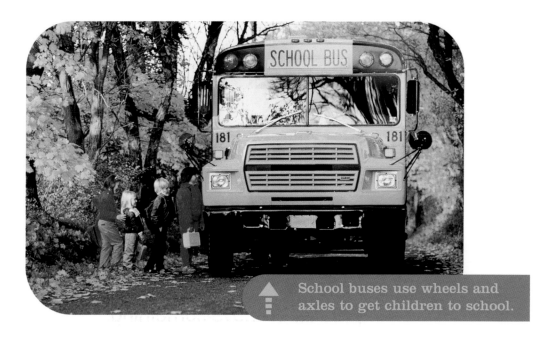

School buses use wheels and axles to get children to school.

The wheel and axle helps with many different jobs all over the world.

Web Sites

To learn more about **Wheels and Axles**, visit ABDO Publishing Company on the World Wide Web. Web site links about **Wheels and Axles** are featured on our Book Links page. These links are routinely monitored and updated to provide the most current information available.

www.abdopublishing.com

Important **Words**

angle the shape made by two straight lines or surfaces meeting in a point.

effort an attempt to lift or move something.

force a push or pull against resistance.

mechanical advantage the way simple machines make work easier. Using a simple machine to help with a task means less, or different, effort is needed to do a job. The same job would require more effort without the help of a simple machine.

resistance something that works against or opposes.

Index